Napkin
Folds

Napkin
Folds

Heide Hellwage-Schmidt

(Translated from the German by Philip Schmitz)

BARNES
&NOBLE
BOOKS
NEW YORK

CONTENTS

NAPKIN FOLDS

Flat, Laid Designs

Upright Designs

Elegant Napkins

Napkins With Decorations or Accessories

DEAR READER,

There are many things

we enjoy remembering. Festive gatherings within our circle of friends or family often number among our cherished memories. Or perhaps we recall a delicious meal we enjoyed at a resort, which recaptures the feeling of being on vacation. Usually, we also recollect exactly what we had to eat on such occasions, even though it might not have been all that special. By comparison, we might have difficulty remembering what was on the menu for the last two weeks.

It's not hard

to find the reason for this. For example, take an acquaintance who has been inspired by her travels to faraway places and hosts the perfect Japanese dinner. Everything is just perfect, from the food right down to the shiny black rice bowls and the hot, moist towels she offers to refresh her guests. Granted, you may be sitting on chairs – out of deference to your knees – but other than that, the illusion is perfect.

That is the reason this birthday celebration will still be remembered several years later. It is well known that we also feast with our eyes, and this hostess knew how to engage all of our senses.

And that is what this book is all about: all the things required to make not only the food but all the "trimmings" perfect too. It includes, for example, selecting and combining the right table linens and dishes, composing perfect place settings and finally, adding napkins as table decorations.

In the 17th-century napkins were already "artistically folded to decorate the table." The year 1894 even saw the publication of two books on the subject: *Festive Table Settings* and *An Illustrated Napkin Album*. So there is nothing new about sophisticated dining, although it was surely never as widespread as it is today.

An informal survey among young people actually found that they view napkins foremost as a form of decorative expression, while the napkin's strictly practical use ranked among the "also-rans." Perhaps this reflects a reaction to fast food in cardboard containers, self-service restaurants and eating on the run.

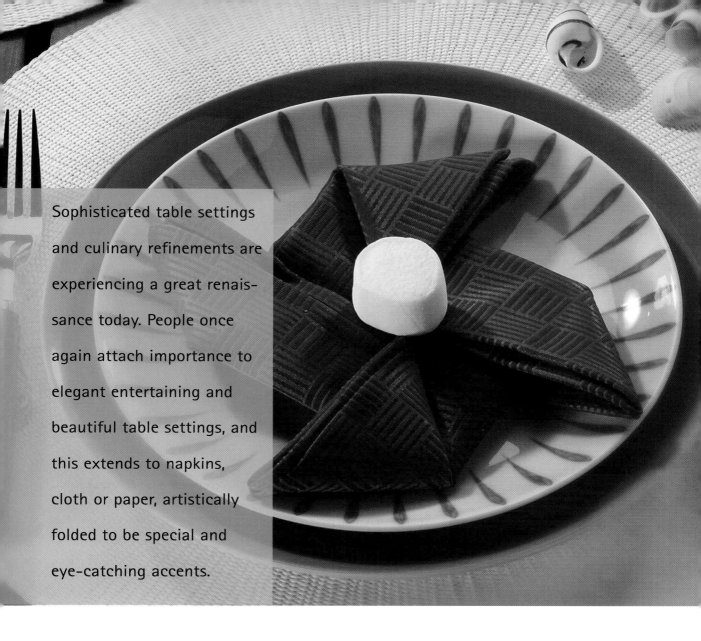

Sophisticated table settings and culinary refinements are experiencing a great renaissance today. People once again attach importance to elegant entertaining and beautiful table settings, and this extends to napkins, cloth or paper, artistically folded to be special and eye-catching accents.

In keeping with the trend this book offers many ideas for creating individual table settings. All of the patterns were folded with cloth napkins, although most can also be made with non-wovens or paper napkins. Cloth napkins should be washed prior to first use; light starch will make them hold their shape better. When ironing, be sure not to distort the shape of the napkin; all corners should be square. Often, though, small irregularities can be adjusted during folding.

If upright forms don't work with a certain material, switch to a flat design instead, rather than resorting to artificial means: this is no place for pins, tape or glue. Try your best to make decorations and napkin rings an integral part of your creation; there must be room for them on the table when they are set aside.

Let the suggestions on the following pages serve as your inspiration. Some of the folds look complicated, but they are easy to reproduce using the photos and step-by-step directions. Your success the next time you entertain will be worth the small investment.

Nowadays, a properly set table must include a napkin. But that was not always the case. Prevailing customs and table manners have changed over the course of history. What was once a privilege of the rich and powerful is now commonplace for one and all.

ETIQUETTE OVER THE CENTURIES

As long as mankind led a nomadic existence, people collected berries and roots and consumed them right on the spot. Occasionally, they would kill an animal, which they ate raw. Only after the discovery of fire did they settle in one place.

The flames, which also offered protection from wild animals at night, were hard to kindle, needed tending, and could not be carried from place to place.

The realization that roasting meat over fire made it tastier and more digestible may have marked the beginnings of culinary tradition.

Meat for roasting was skewered and suspended over the fire using two forked branches. In order not to burn one's fingers, one had to either let the meat cool off or grasp it with a piece of hide or thick leaves. It would be going too far to speak of this as the birth of the napkin, but it might have happened that way.

In addition to supplying the body with the necessary nutrition, eating has always offered an occasion to socialize. The Romans called their banquets *convivium*, which translates as "living together," and thus places the social aspect in the foreground. Cicero attempted to persuade his friend Paetus to attend a banquet by emphasizing that the culinary pleasures were only secondary. For him conviviality, the mental relaxation and the opportunity for pleasant conversation, were the main draw.

The Greeks on the other hand called their feasts *syndeipnion*, which means "eating together." The use of cutlery was not common, which is why the Greeks already used napkins. Usually each guest received two, one for the mouth and one for the hands.

During the age of the Renaissance, in the 14th to 16th centuries, meals served to satisfy a wide range of needs.

The idea was to appeal to both intellect and palate.

Over the course of history etiquette evolved. Primarily among the wealthy and powerful, the manner in which a meal was taken came to represent status and allowed them to flaunt their social standing and disassociate themselves from commoners.

Naturally, both history books and oral tradition are mainly concerned with feasts and have little to report about simple, everyday meals. For example, the grave furnishings of an Egyptian noblewoman indicate that a banquet in approximately 2800 BC consisted of 10 types of meat, 16 different baked goods, 6 vintages of wine, 4 kinds of beer and 11 sorts of fruit. Little is known about how such feasts progressed, but murals depicting female dancers and flutists in transparent attire lead us to believe that there was no lack of entertainment.

The perfectly appointed medieval table from a miniature created in 1470.

Historical reports of table customs in Greece are more detailed. Until the fifth century BC, meals were very simple, consisting mainly of bread and wine, porridges, olives and a little meat. The Greeks sat at a table, although the use of cutlery was still unknown.

Based on various influences from Sicily and Asia Minor, eating customs gradually changed. Men, generally in pairs, now lay on chaises the same height as the table and leaned on their elbows – hardly a comfortable position by today's standards. Women had it better. They could still sit at a table on chairs. Soup was either eaten with spoons or ladled up with a hollowed out piece of bread, on which one also wiped one's hands. Instead of water and towel, perfumed clay was used.

Baron Adolf Knigge, whose name became synonymous with perfect manners.

KNIGGE.

The Romans enjoyed drying their hands on the hair of their female slaves, although they were already acquainted with the use of napkins *(mappa)* and finger bowls. Their eating customs conjure up visions of corpulent senators reclining on chaises and consuming unbelievable amounts of food. The wealthy had themselves carried in litters from one banquet to the next. Often the Romans could no longer tell what they were eating because the taste of food was masked by exotic spices, honey and candied fruits. The presentation of food was paramount, so it is not surprising that the use of peacock feathers was common in the late days of Rome. The feathers were also used to tickle up the contents of the stomach and make room for the next meal.

Our ancestors among the Germanic tribes were a proud people known for negotiating and dealmaking during meals. The prime necessity was to clear one's plate and empty the cup. At banquets in ruling houses, the tables were covered with shining linen. It was always woven by the matron of the house, even if it was the Queen herself, so everyone had to go to great lengths to avoid staining the valuable cloth. Punishment for dirtying the tablecloth was having to sing a long song – raising the question of who was really punished in such cases. But we can assume that the presentations were welcome, for the Germanic people loved nothing so much as song and merriment at table.

In the Middle Ages uncouth behavior was gradually replaced by more refined table manners when, in the 11th century, ladies were also allowed to participate at meals.

At first men and women were separated at the table, but soon a "colorful mix" became the custom. Each knight was seated next to a lady who was his dining partner; generally both ate from a shared

Elderly gentlemen awash in merriment, depicted in a late 19th century painting.

bowl and drank from the same cup.

As a rule, one ate with one's fingers which were washed before and after the meal. One servant would hold out a bowl, while a second poured water from a pitcher over the hands of the guest. Towels to dry off were draped around the servant's neck. Tablecloths were mostly unknown in this age, not to mention napkins, which were only introduced in the 14th-15th century. For the master of the manor, his family and honored guests – who often sat higher than the others – a cloth was sometimes brought to the table for wiping hands and mouth. It was considered the poorest of form to drink from the cup with greasy lips. To wipe one's eyes or teeth with the cloth was not allowed, and it was absolutely forbidden to blow one's nose in the tablecloth.

The German expression "die Tafel aufheben" (literally: to raise the table) originated during this period. The table itself consisted of boards supported on saw-horses. After the meal the servants simply "raised" the boards, including dishes and any leftover food, and carried them off.

The fork, disfavored as an attribute of the devil, had long been employed in the kitchen but as an eating utensil it was first used exclusively in the Byzantine Empire. In the 16th century Henry III brought forks home from Venice, initially introducing them at the French court as serving forks. Only at the court of the Sun King, where gloves were always worn, was the fork finally also used for eating. Meals were now taken in a separate room. The table was covered with white linen; costly porcelain, silverware and napkins were de rigueur.

Gradually, the lifestyle of the aristocracy was mimicked by the bourgeoisie, where special value was placed on impeccable table manners. When Baron Knigge wrote his book "Über den Umgang mit Menschen" (Practical philosophy of social life; or, The art of conversing with men: after the German of Baron Knigge) in 1788, it became a must on everybody's reading list.

Following the two World Wars table manners became less rigid, which many people deemed the end of Western civilization. But in spite of all the pessimism, cultured dining is today experiencing a renaissance. On a day to day basis, meals are generally somewhat hectic, but on special occasions people believe in pulling out all the stops. From an elaborate menu and exquisite food to elegant cutlery, costly glassware, colorfully coordinated table linens and matching accessories – nowadays an invitation to dinner once again promises to be a joy for all of the senses.

TABLE LINENS AND DISHES

During the age of Charlemagne it was a ruler's prerogative to dine with the tablecloth. The possessions of one king are reported to have included a tablecloth, two bed sheets and a towel. Times have certainly changed.

Strictly speaking, a tabletop of wood, marble or glass does not need a tablecloth because it speaks for itself. As a rule, though, we do not omit the tablecloth because it has a decorative effect, protects the surface of the table and mutes the clatter of dishes and cutlery. The rules for tablecloths are similar to those for clothing:

- They should suit the event and highlight the character of the occasion.
- We should feel comfortable with them.
- We may do as we please, as long as we do not attract the wrong kind of attention.

Tablecloths are available in a wide range of choices, and our selection will be informed by color, material, available tableware, usefulness and, of course, budget.

Concerning color, Brillat-Savarin, the witty author of a theory of gustatory delights *(The physiology of Taste; or, Meditations on Transcendental Gastronomy)* published in 1825, demanded "immaculate white." Nowadays, white is not a poor choice because it emphasizes the festive or official character of the meal and places no restrictions on the selection of tableware or decoration. Even in combination with white napkins and white tableware it does not have to be boring because one can use colorful accents such as flower decorations. In addition, the food is shown to its full advantage.

White tablecloths should always be included among the basic appointments. Other than that, the palette ranges from delicate pastels to strong colors, and from opulent patterns to silver and gold colored material. The decisive factors are one's own personal preferences and supply of tableware.

Some porcelain manufacturers offer table linens to match their wares. Decorative elements from the dishes are repeated sometimes throughout the entire tablecloth, sometimes only in the trim. Tablecloths which reflect the predominant color of the decoration, or echo the design in their weave, produce an harmonious effect. Certain rules govern the selection of the material, but they needn't always be strictly followed. Here, too, the maxim holds: if it pleases you, it's permitted. Often breaking the rules can produce uniquely creative table settings, for example using expensive silverware with coarsely textured linen.

For sanitary reasons laundry settings for tablecloths should be at least 60° C. Linen and cotton, the most common materials, can even be washed at 95° C, which is an advantage when there are stubborn stains. Modal and Viscose, synthetic fibers manufactured from cellulose, and polyester are used, frequently in blends. The cotton or linen content provides the necessary absorbency, which is above all important in napkins, while the synthetic fiber makes the material sturdier and easier to care for. Some materials are treated for stain resistance or coated, which is practical for tablecloths but not appropriate for napkins.

Linen has a natural sheen and a somewhat irregular weave which goes well with more rustic dishes. More refined are cotton and cotton blends, from which shiny damask with its patterned weave and Jacquard are made. Piqué is a new material which is highly structured. Satin looks extremely elegant. In addition, there are tablecloths with open embroidery work which look especially pretty when a differently colored cloth is placed underneath. Hand or machine embroidered monograms are en vogue again, as are scalloped, lace or tasseled edges.

If a dining table is too small, a large sheet of wood can be laid over two sawhorses. These must be covered with long cloths which hang down 35-40 cm. With normal dining tables the tablecloth should drape 25-30 cm over the edge. When using long organza cloths as a decoration over the tablecloth, be sure that the tassels hang down between the place settings.

Tablecloths are offered with matching cloth and sometimes even paper napkins. And although the latter are practical, environmental concerns make cloth napkins – a must for stylish table settings – preferable even for everyday use. They should not be too thick and should be made of an appropriate material. Organza looks nice, but is impractical; a similar effect can be achieved with delicate Japanese paper napkins. Cloth napkins are usually available in sizes 40 x 40 cm or 50 x 50 cm, less frequently 45 x 45 cm. Heirlooms from bygone days are often larger

because they stem from a time when napkins were still worn around the neck. Napkins can be made to order in any size, as can tablecloths for use on irregularly sized tables. As with tablecloths, using white dishes is no mistake. Ever since fashion designers like Versace and Hermès began creating lines of tableware with varying ornamentation, mixing patterns is acceptable when there are not enough pieces available. There are a few guidelines, however, for combining dishes with tablecloths:

- Dishes with colorful patterns look best with table linen in either a solid color or with a woven design in a matching color. Contrasting colors can create a pretty effect, e. g., dark red with green patterned dishware, but be careful. Pure colors often look garish while muted ones are more harmonious.
- Solid colored dishes also work with a colorfully patterned tablecloth; patterned napkins, however, would be too much.

- Mixing patterns is allowed, as long as the result doesn't make your head swim. Remember, small patterns are more easily compatible than large ones.
- Tone on tone color combinations look elegant; for example, a gray tablecloth, white porcelain with silver trim, suitable glasses, stainless steel cutlery and silver-gray napkins. A floral arrangement or table runner of a contrasting color would add an element of excitement.

THE PERFECT PLACE SETTING

It is not only permissible, but also makes good sense to question traditions. For example, is it still necessary at all to set the table according to certain rules? Primarily it is helpful for guests, and aesthetic demands are also met.

Setting a table correctly offers clear advantages in addition to creating an aesthetic effect. The cutlery offers an overview of the coming menu, and guests can pace their appetite to the sequence of courses so they do not have to begin declining food when the main dish arrives. When exotic food is served, one also immediately knows which utensil to use.

During a meal with several courses, stylish table settings create a festive mood. But aesthetics should be informed by function. Floral arrangements which obstruct the view, candles which cause burns as one serves oneself, and plate or cup decorations which cannot be laid aside are irritating. Correctly selected accessories allow the guests to integrate them into the overall table decoration. But first, the question of space: each person needs at least 50 cm; 60 to 70 cm are ideal. There should be room for a chair without crowding.

The place setting consists of everything necessary for the meal ahead: dishes, cutlery, glasses and a napkin.

A charger plate is set first if available, for according to an old rule the guest must always be seated in front of a plate. Nowadays, though, a special charger plate is more a decorative element; a flat dinner plate fills the purpose just

bowl could be set in the same place, although as a rule this is brought out with dessert.

If shellfish will be served in the shell, a small finger bowl is placed to the left of the plate in addition to a second napkin.

Cutlery is set in the order in which it will be used, from the outside working in. Here, the distance from the edge of the table is two fingers.

It will be appreciated as an especially considerate gesture if left-handed guests can begin eating without having to switch the cutlery. In general, though, the table is set for right-handed people, with knives and soup spoon to the right of the plate and forks to the left. Knives and spoons are arranged precisely parallel to the edge of the table, while forks are staggered to the upper left. The knife edge always points toward the plate, the tines of the forks face up, and the bowls of the spoons face down.

as well. The first plate is laid one finger width from the edge of the table. The smaller appetizer plate or soup plate is placed on top if a warm appetizer is to follow. On top of that comes an artistically folded napkin. On principle, no more than two dishes are ever placed on top of each other.

If bread and butter will be served, an appropriate plate is set on the left, next to the forks. In a pinch a saucer will do. The butter spreader or a small appetizer knife is laid parallel to the other knives to the right of the plate.

If salad will be served as a side dish to the main course, the salad plate is set on the left-hand side above the forks. If the salad will be served as a course unto itself, a plate is not set. A small desert

If at all possible, cutlery for dessert should be set after the main course when the table has been cleared. Otherwise, the dessert knife lies above the plate and the fork above that. A spoon, if needed, lies above the fork, the handle pointing to the right. The handle of the dessert fork points to the left.

A knife rest for holding a used knife is positioned diagonally over the dinner knife, but can be omitted if separate cutlery is set for every course.

Fish cutlery is always preset, while any special utensils are offered as the course is served. Other than that, lobster, escargot, oyster and fondue forks, as well as caviar knives and caviar spoons, go on the right, while crab utensils, escargot tongs and lobster crackers belong on the left.

Two identical pieces should never be placed next to each other. Recommendations vary concerning the number of pieces on either side – sometimes three, sometimes four. The best solution is to be guided by the amount of room available and by one's own personal inventory. When different sets of cutlery must be combined, setting them sequentially with each dish is recommended. Cutlery is also used as sign language:

- Crossed on the plate: "I'm taking a short break, but I'm not finished yet."
- Held in the hands, pointing toward the middle of the plate, the heel of your palm resting on the table: "I would enjoy having some more of these delicacies."
- Lying next to each other, pointing downward and to the right: "I'm finished. The table may be cleared."

- Knife and fork propped on the edge of the plate with the handles resting on the table: This is a sign of poor table manners and should be avoided if one is trying to make a good impression.

If the goal is utter perfection, the wine glass for the main course is placed at the tip of the dinner knife. For example, in the case of roast venison, this would involve a red wine goblet. If someone prefers white wine, Rosé or beer, all three types of glasses are set, space permitting. A water tumbler should never be lacking because water neutralizes the gustatory nerves and renders them more receptive. Additionally, drinking water is thirst quenching and helps control alcohol levels. The water glass is positioned to the far right. A tall glass or a shorter wine glass will serve the purpose.

There are nicely shaped, neutral stem glasses available today in which almost anything can be served, but certain beverages will only develop their full aroma in very special glassware. Likewise, coffee and tea also taste best in a proper cup. When setting the table, the cup is placed diagonally above and to the right of the cake plate, the cup handle pointing to the right. The spoon rests on the saucer with the handle pointing to the right and extending over the saucer edge. Cake forks are placed either next to the plate or laid diagonally across it, and help with draping a dainty napkin. For coffee or tea, the napkin should not be too large or too thick. Following the Viennese coffee-house tradition, a water glass may be placed to the left of the cup. When applying all of these rules, though, one should always bear in mind that less is often more. An overloaded table makes the same impression as an overloaded plate: it can ruin one's appetite. And if there is no room on the table for the aperitif glass – well, standing around casually in a group, glass in hand, is nicer anyway.

USING THE NAPKIN

The French word for napkin, "serviette", originally meant an "object needed for serving." Today napkins play an additional, decorative role, but it's also important to know how to use one correctly.

A medieval German rule of etiquette read, "Have a woman, maid or serving girl tie a cloth around you." And in the 16th century the rule was, " . . . you must not get your fingers so dirty that you soil the napkin when you wipe them . . . " In Italy and France 500 years ago it was considered good form to first clean one's fingers with a piece of bread, which was left on the plate, before wiping them on a napkin – which was to be returned without being excessively soiled.

There have always been rules for how to use a napkin, although today they have changed somewhat. For example, tying the napkin around one's neck or stuffing it under one's collar is no longer permissible, unless spaghetti is served. In southern France and Italy, though, diners take a more relaxed view of the matter and one should decide what is appropriate on a case-by-case basis.

A napkin (in German they are also known as "mouth napkins") has two functions. First, one always uses it to dab one's mouth before taking a drink so that no lip marks are left on the glass. Secondly, the napkin can be used to shield one's clothing from crumbs, etc., which drop down. No matter how beautifully it is folded, it must be opened at the beginning of the meal. It is meant to be used, and has fulfilled its aesthetic function beforehand. If blossoms, branches, sweets or such have been integrated into the fold, they are now removed and placed above the plate, or possibly even added to the other table decorations.

The correct location for a napkin is in one's lap. It is practical to fold the upper third under, which prevents the napkin from slipping off so easily. The underside of the fold can also be used to dab one's mouth without remnants of food becoming visible or touching one's clothing.

When leaving the table during the meal, place the napkin to the left of the plate, loosely folded and with any "evidence of use" facing in – although Americans lay the napkin on the chair. This also holds true for paper napkins; it is considered poor form to roll them into a ball and lay them in the leftover sauce.

When shellfish such as shrimps are served in the shell, they may be eaten with one's fingers. But then there needs to be a finger bowl to the left of the plate, together with a second napkin which is used to dry one's hands. It should then be loosely folded and placed underneath the finger bowl.

Napkin
Folds

Regardless of whether you choose flat folds or upright forms, whether you would like to enhance folded napkins with accessories or highlight the beauty of elegant materials – you are sure to find the right solution for every occasion among the 50 napkin designs on the following pages.

ENCHANTED FLOWER

1. Open the napkin (right side down) and fold all four corners to the middle. Smooth out any creases.

2. Working on the same side of the material, repeat step one with the newly created corners. Turn the napkin over.

3. For a third time, fold all four corners into the middle.

4. Firmly hold the middle and pull out the points on the bottom underneath each of the corners; this creates the filled flower petals.

5. Pull the corners on the bottom between the flower petals half-way out.

Dimensions: 40 x 40 cm. Materials: starched cloth napkins (for example, structured satin) or paper; non-wovens only conditionally

This pattern looks best when the napkin has a silky shine. If the center pops up too much it can be weighed down with a seashell, a snail shell or a glass ball. Snail shells are particularly fitting if escargots will be served as an appetizer.

KNOT

This pattern might be used at a garden party for a decorative display of napkin and cutlery.

1. Open the napkin (right side down) and fold the two opposing corners to the middle.

2. Fold the creases created in Step 1 in to the middle again.

3. Fold in half lengthwise.

4. Cross one end over the other, with the longer end on top.

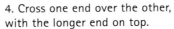

5. Use the longer end to tie a knot around the shorter. Pull the end points out.

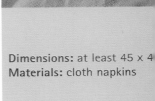

Dimensions: at least 45 x 4
Materials: cloth napkins

SURPRISE PACKAGE

Dimensions: all sizes. Materials: either cloth or non-woven napkins

1. Open the napkin (right side facing down) and position it diagonally. Fold the bottom corner up, forming a triangle.

2. Fold both corners of the triangle up to the top corner, forming a square once again.

3. Turn the napkin over. The closed corner now points down.

4. Fold the lower corner up to the top, forming a triangle.

5. Fold the left and right corners diagonally upward and across the center so that they extend beyond the edge of the triangle. Turn the napkin over.

6. Spread the flaps to either side and open them slightly.

7. Fold down the two top layers of the inner diamond.

Little surprises for Sunday brunch can be tucked into this very special package. Basically, any material can be used, but a tightly woven, well-structured napkin will make an especially good impression.

Precision is the key to this fold. The points must come to meet exactly in the middle and may even overlap slightly. Weight the center point with a sweet.

WINDMILL

1. Open the napkin (right side facing down), and fold the lower half up.

2. Fold in half again, forming a small square.

3. Fold in each of the two opposing corners (top right and bottom left) exactly to the mid-point.

4. Fold the upper left and lower right corners to the back, exactly to the mid-point.

5. Fold the two opposing corners exactly to the mid-point. Turn the napkin over.

6. Fold the left and right corners in to the mid-point.

7. While holding the mid-point, pull out the open layers of material underneath the most recently formed triangles. Turn over.

8. Holding the mid-point firmly once again, pull out the open layers of material under the triangles.

Dimensions:
45 x 45 cm
Materials:
well–starched
cloth napkin, as
well as non–
wovens or paper

DOUBLE CORNET

When time is of the essence, this equally simple and sophisticated double cornet can be folded in a jiffy.

1. Open the napkin (right side down), arrange it diagonally and fold it into a triangle from the bottom up.

2. Determine the mid-point of the baseline and initially fold each of the two corners up about one-third of the way.

3. Roll both sides up toward the middle.

4. If the cornet is to stay round, fold the tips back inside.

Dimensions: 40 x 40 cm or 45 x 45 cm
Materials: starched cloth napkins as well as non-wovens or paper

This pattern is easy to fold but still impressive. Our photo shows how flowers scattered over the table perfectly complement napkin and tableware.

FLAT CORNET

Dimensions: 40 x 40 cm
Materials: starched cloth napkins as well as non-wovens or paper

1. Open the napkin (right side down) and arrange it diagonally.

2. Fold the top corner down to form a triangle.

3. While holding down the bottom point fold the left and right corners diagonally up across the middle.

4. Turn the napkin over and open slightly.

FISH

Dimensions: 40 x 40 cm or smaller
Materials: sturdy cloth napkins as well as non-wovens or paper

1. Open the napkin (right side down) and arrange it diagonally.

2. Fold the top corner down to form a triangle.

3. Fold the upper edge down about 5 cm. Turn napkin over.

4. Use the thumb of one hand to hold down the top center point. Using the other hand, fold the left and right triangle points around the thumb and diagonally down to the opposite side.

5. Turn the entire pattern over and adjust the "fins" of the napkin-fish.

This is just the right design for an elegant fish or seafood dish. Damask napkins as seen in the photograph are perfect for such culinary delights.

GEISHA

1. Open the napkin (right side down) and fold both sides toward the middle, extending about 2 cm over the center line.

2. Fold 2-3 cm of the lower edge upwards; consider ironing it.

3. Fold the lower third of the napkin upward.

4. Fold down both top corners of this third in along an imaginary center line.

5. Fold 2 cm of the top edge to the back.

6. Now also fold the upper third toward the back to just below the point of the triangle.

7. Fold the sides in toward the "collar." This forms two triangles on the top edge.

8. Fold the top edge toward the back, forming the "sleeves."

Dimensions: at least 50 x 50 cm
Materials: : lightly starched cloth napkins; when using non-wovens or paper, the middle fold must be ironed flat.

The "Geisha" is especially striking when both napkin and ambience have Far Eastern accents. This fold requires large napkins.

For this pattern we recommend a napkin with a striped border to underscore the diagonal folds.

DIAGONAL

1. Open the napkin (right side down) and fold the bottom half up.

2. Fold in half from the right forming a small square with the closed corner in the lower left.

3. Fold the upper right corner of the top layer down to its opposing corner; this forms a diagonal.

4. About 3 cm below the diagonal, fold the same corner back up.

5. Tuck the corner under the diagonal.

6. Fold the next corner down at a distance of about 3 cm from the diagonal.

7. Tuck this corner under the diagonal as well.

8. Fold both sides to the back.

Dimensions: 45 x 45 cm. Materials: all napkin types

Whenever it makes sense to offer two napkins,
this fold is the best choice.

DOUBLE DIAGONAL

1. Open two differently colored napkins of equal size and lay them – right sides touching – one on top of the other.

2. Fold the napkins in half from the bottom up.

3. Fold the napkins in half from the right. (The open corners are at the top right.)

4. Fold the top three layers of cloth down to the lower left corner. Press firmly along the diagonal crease this creates.

Dimensions: 45 x 45 cm or 50 x 50 cm
Materials: thin cloth napkins, non-wovens only when used together with paper napkins. Use only solid colored paper napkins.

5. Open the next two layers and fold them down at a distance of about 4 cm from the diagonal. Tuck the small triangle underneath the diagonal.

6. Fold this flap down.

7. Fold the napkins in half toward the back.

Dimensions: 40 x 40 cm or 45 x 45 cm
Materials: lightly starched cloth napkins; if using non-woven or paper napkins the center folds must be ironed flat.

CHRISTMAS TREE

1. Open the napkin (right side down) and fold in half vertically.

2. Mark the middle of the top edge and fold both corners in on a diagonal.

3. Fold one corner in, extending over the imaginary center line.

4. Repeat with the other corner. A triangle has been formed.

5. At the base of the triangle fold the napkin up toward the top.

6. About 5 cm above the bottom crease fold the straight piece back down again.

7. Fold the lower right corner inward extending over the imaginary center line.

8. Repeat the process with the lower left corner, then turn the napkin over.

This pattern requires measuring by the eye because there are no creases to use as guidelines. It is important that the "trunk" of the little napkin tree does not become too long. Small Christmassy shapes of stamped brass scattered over table and napkins would be suitable decorations.

POINTED CORNET

Dimensions: 45 x 45 cm. Materials: sturdy or well-starched cloth napkins as well as thick paper or non-wovens

1. Fold the napkin in half from the top down, wrong sides of the material touching.

2. Determine the mid-point and roll the upper right corner over the center line to the upper left corner.

3. The lower right corner should come to rest exactly on top of the lower left corner.

4. When the napkin is entirely rolled up, fold both right and left corners up high enough to secure the open left corner.

5. Form a hat and stand it upright.

With the pointed cornet, the material determines the effect. This design is very attractive – and not only in classical damask, as can be seen in the photographs.

The Noblesse fold is excellent for large napkins. The hems must not be too wide when the points are turned down (as shown in the variation below).

NOBLESSE

Dimensions: 50 x 50 cm. **Materials:** lightly starched cloth napkins

1. Open the napkin (right side down), arrange it diagonally and fold the bottom corner up to form a triangle.

2. Fold the right and left corners up to the top middle point to form a diamond.

3. Turn the diamond over so that the closed point is on top. Fold the bottom points up to the top.

4. Open the top triangles and fold them along the baseline to form diamonds.

5. Fold the bottom points back up again.

6. Turn the napkin over. Bring both corners around to the front and interlock them.

7a. Set the napkin upright and spread the side pockets open.

7b. (Variation) Fold down the top two layers of material.

Naturally, this well-known, classic fold could not be left out. The simple fan can be created in any size and from basically any material. But one thing always applies: the larger and stiffer the napkin used, the more impressive the result.

SIMPLE FAN

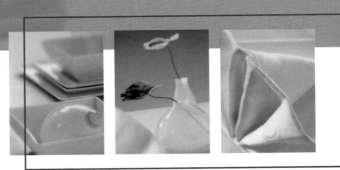

Dimensions: 50 x 50 cm
Materials: well-starched cloth napkins

1. Open the napkin (right side down) and fold it in half from left to right.

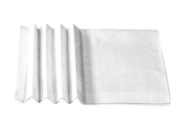

2. Rotate 90° to the right and, beginning from one of the narrow ends, create accordion folds about 2 cm wide until slightly past the mid-point.

3. Fold the accordion and the smooth part in half by turning it underneath. The accordion remains on the outside.

4. Fold the smooth part up to meet the accordion.

5. Fold the upper right corner downward and to the left and slip underneath the first accordion fold.

6. Fan the accordion folds open and stand upright.

SCALLOPED FAN

Dimensions: 55 x 55 cm
Materials: starched cloth napkins (especially attractive with lace); non-woven or paper napkins are also appropriate.

1. Open the napkin (right side down) and fold in half from the bottom up.

2. Fold in half again, from the bottom up.

3. Beginning at the narrow end, form accordion folds about 3 cm wide; iron the folds when finished.

4. Fan the napkin open in such a way that the closed edge forms the outside perimeter; stand upright.

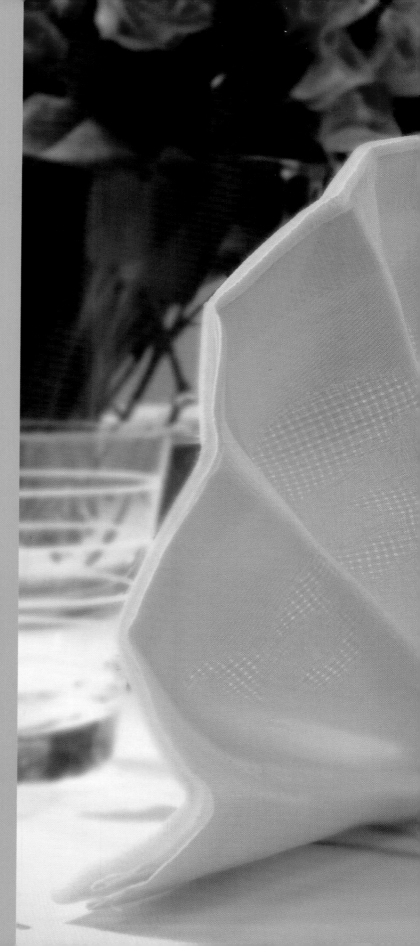

This fold can be varied any way you wish. The open edges may also form the outside perimeter. If you are serving tea, use a napkin with a Japanese design – your guests will immediately think of a Japanese tea ceremony.

SNOWDROPS

To ensure that this pattern results in real "Snowdrops," make your folds precise. It is important that the right side faces in at first, as the napkin is unfolded again.

Dimensions: 40 x 40 cm
Materials: cloth napkins, as well as non-wovens or paper

1. Open the napkin (right side facing up) and fold in half. Press down firmly on the crease.

2. Open the napkin.

3. Fold the napkin in half from left to right. Press down firmly on the crease and open the napkin again (right side still facing up).

4. Fold the napkin in half horizontally so that the top half becomes the back. Push the upper right corner in to the center line.

5. Repeat with the upper left corner.

6. Set napkin upright and bend points outward.

This design looks much more complicated than it actually is. If you are using a linen napkin, be sure to press down the corners especially hard.

STRELITZIA

1. Open the napkin (right side down) and fold it in half, first from the top, and then from the side, forming a small square.

2. Arrange the square so the open edges are on the bottom.

3. Fold the open edges up to form a triangle.

4. Fold the right corner down to the center line. Repeat with the left corner.

5. Fold the whole napkin in half toward the back.

6. Fold the two bottom points in and secure them firmly in the pleat.

7. Stand upright and pull three of the inner corners upward to form points.

Dimensions: 40 x 40 cm
Materials: starched cloth napkins; paper napkins

Coarsely structured napkins are a must for creating the porcupine, but be sure that the texture is still pleasantly soft. When in doubt, omit the starch.

PORCUPINE

1. Open the napkin (right side down) and fold it in half.

2. Fold in half again and arrange the napkin so that the open edges point up.

3. Fold the top four corners down to form a triangle.

4. About 2 cm from the crease, fold the top layer of material back up again.

5. Repeat this process with the other layers of material at ever widening distances from the crease.

6. Fold the entire napkin vertically down the middle toward the back.

7. Set napkin upright and gently pull the points forward.

Dimensions: 40 x 40 cm
Materials: lightly starched cloth napkin

SOLITAIRE

Dimensions: all sizes
Materials: suitable for all napkin types; light starch

1. Open the napkin (right side down) and fold in half from the top down.

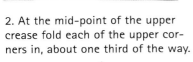

2. At the mid-point of the upper crease fold each of the upper corners in, about one third of the way.

3. Fold the corners in one more time.

4. Perform a third fold, this time along the center line.

5. Fold the napkin in half along the center line.

6. Fold the loose bottom triangles upward on both sides.

7. Stand the napkin upright.

A solitaire refers to a gemstone which has been set by itself and is just as exquisite as this napkin form. If you decide on this fold, keep table decorations relatively flat and under-stated so that the elegance of this sleek pyramid can be appreciated.

LUXOR

1. Open the napkin (right side down) and fold in half from left to right.

2. Determine the mid-point of the top edge and fold in both upper corners to meet along the imaginary center line.

3. Fold this triangle down and turn the napkin over.

4. As in Step 2, fold in both top corners.

5. Fold the smooth part of the napkin upward at the base of the triangle.

6. Fold this part down again at a distance of about 1 cm from the crease. Turn the napkin over and iron it. Fold the smooth part back up to the top and create accordion folds.

7. Slip the accordion folds underneath the diamond. Press firmly and fan open the ends.

8. Turn the napkin over and stand it upright.

Dimensions: 50 x 50 cm.
Materials: starched cloth napkins

This form requires ironing. The corners of
the diamonds are secured by the horizontal
folds.

The color and structure of the napkin used in this example are ideal for this upright design.

DUCK

1. Open the napkin (right side down) and arrange it diagonally. Fold the corners on both sides in to meet along an imaginary center line.

2. Fold the bottom corner upward, forming an acute-angled triangle.

Dimensions: 40 x 40 cm.
Materials: lightly starched cloth napkins, as well as non-wovens and paper

3. Fold the bottom part up slightly more than one-third of the way.

4. Fold the entire napkin in half from left to right.

5. . Grasp the top point, the "duck's neck," about halfway down and bend the point horizontally to the left.

6. Fold the lower right corner upward to the left to meet the vertical crease. Repeat on the back.

7. Stand the duck upright and interlock the two rear points.

Here, material and napkin design blend harmoniously with the Oriental mood of the festive table setting. This form is especially attractive in gold satin.

DUCK BILL SHOE

1. Open the napkin (right side down) and fold in half laterally.

2. Fold in half from the top to form a small square. Arrange so that the open edges are pointing down.

3. Fold the top three corners upward, each about 1 cm away from the one before.

4. Fold the left and right corners down and to the middle.

5. Fold the entire napkin in half vertically toward the back.

6. Grasping the form in the middle, pull the lower triangle out some-what to the left and interlock the corners to the right.

7. Pull the triangle all the way out, then fold it inward and over the back edge of the shoe.

8. Gently pull the points upward.

Dimensions: 45 x 45 cm, better 55 x 55 cm
Materials: somewhat sturdier cloth napkins

The Lily numbers among the classical napkin folds. Its appearance depends greatly on the material selected. Portrayed here is a napkin of a struc-tured material with a silky sheen, machine embroidery and a scalloped edge. The combination of a real lily in a dark vase is especially stylish.

LILY

1. Open the napkin (right side down), arrange it diagonally and fold the top corner down to form a triangle.

Dimensions: 40 x 40 cm
Materials: cloth napkins (very decorative with lace edges), as well as non-wovens and paper napkins

2. Beginning at the middle of the top crease fold the right and left corners down to the lower corner.

3. Fold these two corners back up to the top.

4. Fold about two-thirds of the lower corners upward and slip them under the two triangles.

5. Fold the bottom crease of the napkin upward.

6. Turn the napkin over. Bring the corners on both sides around to the front and interlock them.

7. Bend the points of the triangles down and tuck them under the rim.

The rustic style of this fold goes well with a hearty snack. Or, you can also use the boot at Christmastime – in red with a pine branch.

BOOT

1. Open the napkin (right side down) and fold in half from the top down. The crease should be on top.

2. Fold the bottom third up.

3. Fold the top third down.

4. Fold the right end down along the center line. Repeat this with the left side.

5. Fold the left half onto the right. Turn the napkin over and rotate 90° to the left.

6. Fold the lower part in and turn it down.

7. Bring the turned part back up and tuck it into the triangle.

Dimensions: 50 x 50 cm. Materials: sturdy cloth napkins, as well as non-wovens and paper

Dimensions: 40 x 40 cm or 45 x 45 cm
Materials: all napkin types

PEEL OFF

1. Open the napkin (right side down), arrange it diagonally and fold it up from the bottom to form a triangle.

2. Fold the left and right corners up to the top corner forming a diamond.

3. Fold the lower corner of the diamond up, but leave a margin of about 3 cm.

4. Fold the corner that now lies on top back down again, extending about 1 cm beyond the baseline.

5. Fold both of the two-layered points down as well.

6. Turn the napkin over. Bring the right and left corners to the front and interlock them.

7. Stand the napkin upright and bend the three points upward slightly.

This elegant form is reminiscent of a half-peeled fruit. The effect is created by the folds extending somewhat beyond the baseline. "Peel Off" can be made using all napkin types with no trouble.

TEA FOR TWO

1. Open the napkin and, starting from the edge, create accordion folds approximately 3 cm wide.

Dimensions: all sizes may be used
Materials: lightly starched cloth napkins, as well as non-wovens and paper

2. Fold both sides to the middle allowing them to overlap slightly. Consider ironing the napkin at this point.

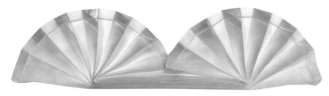

3. Press down firmly on the inside creases and open each fan.

In the photograph, this fold harmonizes perfectly because the low arches of the napkin are combined with the extremely shallow teacups. Colored paper napkins must be patterned on both sides for this fold.

This fold allows variations. When using very thick napkins, Step 6 can be omitted. The individual points can be draped however you fancy.

DOUBLE RIMMED MITER

1. Open the napkin (right side down) and fold in half from the bottom.

2. Fold in half again and arrange the napkin so that the open points are facing down.

3. Fold the three top layers up, one after the other, leaving a margin of 1–2 cm between each.

4. Fold the bottom corner up to meet the bottom crease.

5. Fold up the bottom flap.

6. Fold up the bottom crease.

7. Turn the napkin over. Bring the left and right corners around to the front and interlock them.

8. Stand the napkin upright and pull the individual layers of material gently to the front and downward.

Dimensions: 45 x 45 cm or 50 x 50 cm
Materials: all napkin types

The simple peacock may be folded
ahead of time and stored flat. When it
is time to set the table, it only needs
to be fanned open.

SIMPLE PEACOCK

1. Open the napkin (right side
up), and fold in half from the
bottom up.

2. Fold the top layer of material in
half from the top down. Turn the
napkin over and repeat this step.

3. Starting at the narrow end,
form accordion folds 4 cm wide.

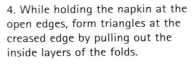

4. While holding the napkin at the
open edges, form triangles at the
creased edge by pulling out the
inside layers of the folds.

Dimensions: 45 x 45 cm
or 55 x 55 cm
Materials: well-starched
cloth napkins

5. Finally, carefully fan the napkin open.

The light, floating gracefulness of this fold is best emphasized by placing the napkin in tall narrow transparent glasses.

DRAGONFLY

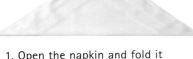

1. Open the napkin and fold it into a triangle (the right side of the material is on the outside).

Dimensions: 40 x 40 cm
Materials: sturdy or well-starched cloth napkins, as well as strong paper or non-wovens.

2. Starting at the baseline, form accordion folds 2 cm wide.

3. Fold in the middle in such a way that the creased edge faces outward and insert the napkin into a glass.

A light, delicate design which is a good choice when serving coffee. But be sure to use napkins made of very thin material, otherwise they will not fit between the tines of a fork.

BUTTERFLY

1. Open the napkin and beginning in one corner form accordion folds about 2 cm wide.

2. Insert the middle of the butterfly into a three pronged cake fork.

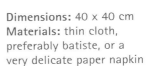

Dimensions: 40 x 40 cm
Materials: thin cloth, preferably batiste, or a very delicate paper napkin

Fassile means "simple" (derived from the French word "facile"), and indeed, this design is exceedingly easy to fold. Pretty napkin rings, strings of pearls or snappy accessories are shown off to their best.

FASSILE

Dimensions: 45 x 45 cm or 55 x 55 cm
Materials: suitable for all napkin types

1. Open the napkin (right side down) and fold it in half.

2. Fold the napkin lengthwise into accordion folds.

3. Fold the entire napkin in half, hold it together with a napkin ring or a string of pearls, and fan open.

FAIRY HAT

Dimensions 40 x 40 cm
Materials: starched cloth napkins,
sturdy non-wovens or paper

1. Open the napkin (right side down) and fold in half from the top down.

2. Determine the midpoint and roll the upper right corner exactly to the centerline.

3. Continue rolling until the right corner is directly above the lower left corner.

4. Fold these two corners up high enough to form a hat. Stand the napkin upright.

5. Decorate the faerie hat with pearl wire.

Shown here is a successful combination of decoration, material, color and form. If you prefer cool colors, select midnight blue for the napkins and tablecloth and silver for the decorations.

The Little Devil is just the right fold for the New Year's Eve menu. Black and red are the colors of choice.

LITTLE DEVIL

Dimensions: 45 x 45 cm or 55 x 55 cm
Materials: suitable for all napkin types

1. Open the napkin (right side down) and fold in half.

2. Fold in half again and arrange the napkin so that the open corners point up.

3. Fold the lower corner up to form a triangle.

4. Determine the middle of the baseline and fold the right corner diagonally upwards so that it extends beyond the edge.

5. Repeat Step 4 with the left corner and then turn the napkin over.

6. Turn down the top two layers, then tuck the next two layers behind the crease. Decorate with feathers in matching colors.

TUXEDO

Since this form lies flat on the plate, it allows table decorations to be fully appreciated. For this reason, ornament the Tuxedo only sparingly, for example with a bow.

1. Open the napkin (right side down), arrange it diagonally, and fold the top down to form a triangle.

2. Fold a flap down from the top crease at least 4 cm. Consider ironing the napkin at this point.

3. Turn the triangle over and, starting about 5 cm from the imaginary middle, fold the right corner down diagonally.

4. Fold the left corner down over the right.

5. Fold the corners on either side around to the back.

Dimensions: 50 x 50 cm. Materials: lightly starched cloth napkins

Little Easter surprises can be hidden on the table either within the head of the napkin rabbit or even between its ears. For this design the material must not be too smooth, otherwise the shape will not hold.

RABBIT

1. Open the napkin (right side down), arrange it diagonally, and fold the bottom up to form a triangle.

2. Fold the left and right corners up to the top point to form a diamond.

Dimensions: 40 x 40 cm or 45 x 45 cm
Materials: suitable for all napkin types

3. Once again, fold the bottom corner up to the top to form a triangle.

4. Bring the corners on both sides around to the front and interlock them.

5. Fold the first two points forward and secure them.

6. Turn the napkin over. Fold the top triangle down (forming the head) and pull the loose points to either side (forming the ears).

MEDALLION

Dimensions: all sizes. Materials: starched cloth napkins or paper napkins, best with an ornamental border.

1. Open the napkin (right side down) and fold all four corners exactly to the center. Turn the napkin over.

2. Once again, fold all four corners to the middle, then turn the napkin over.

3. Fold all four corners to the middle again, turn the napkin over and rotate 45°.

4. Fold the inside right point over the outside right point and then pull it further out.

5. Repeat Step 4 with the three other points.

When the occasion calls for menus or place cards, the
Medallion is the ideal solution. Cloth napkins must be pulled
out somewhat farther at the ends.

CHAPEAU

1. Open the napkin (right side down) and fold in half from the bottom up.

2. Fold the lower right corner up and the upper left corner down so they meet along an imaginary centerline.

3. Turn the napkin over in such a way that the lower left corner becomes the upper right corner.

4. Fold the top crease down halfway.

5. Take out the little triangle underneath the napkin on the upper right and unfold it all the way.

6. Fold the left corner in toward the right, as far as the middle.

7. Fold the triangle from Step 5 back up.

8. Turn the napkin over.

9. Fold the left corner toward the right and slip it under the triangle on the right.

10. Rotate the entire form 180°. Grasp the top crease and then bend the two bottom points outward. Form a hat, raise the inside material slightly and stand upright.

Dimensions: 40 x 40 cm
Materials: lightly starched cloth napkins, as well as non-wovens or paper

This is a wonderful place for little surprises or decorations, like flowers. The finely ribbed texture of the napkin used here emphasizes the clear lines of the design.

Dimensions: 40 x 40 cm. Materials: as thin a napkin as possible

CHOPSTICKS

Using chopsticks, you will find it easy to produce an even, narrow napkin roll. For the meal itself, though, be sure to set a fork as well – just in case.

1. Open the napkin (right side down) and arrange it diagonally.

2. Place the wide end of a chopstick on the bottom corner and roll up the napkin about one-third of the way. Repeatedly pull the chopstick out to one side.

3. Insert the second chopstick into the tube from the other side and push it to the middle.

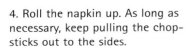

4. Roll the napkin up. As long as necessary, keep pulling the chopsticks out to the sides.

5. Fold in half in the middle, and let the chopsticks peek out of the ends.

Dimensions: 40 x 40 cm.
Materials: all materials may be used although starched batiste napkins are best.

KINGFISHER

1. Open the napkin (right side down) and arrange it diagonally. Fold the corners on both sides in along an imaginary centerline.

2. Fold the bottom corner up, forming an acute-angled triangle.

3. Fold the bottom section up, about one-third of the way. Turn the napkin over.

5. Using both index fingers, fold the two small corners toward the back and middle, forming a triangle.

6. Press thumbs firmly along the edges of the triangle and fold to the left.

7. Fold the entire napkin in half toward the right.

9. Then fold the same corner back to the right again. Perform the last two steps in reverse on the back.

To form the Kingfisher
successfully it is impor-
tant to press the creases
firmly.

4. Fold the top point down to the horizontal. Form a fold about 1 cm wide, then fold the point up again. Turn the napkin over.

8. Fold the lower right corner to the left until it meets the vertical crease.

10. Place the fold in a cup or glass. For greater stability, the bottom point may be bent to one side.

FOLDED NAPKIN RING

There is hardly a more gracious way to focus attention on a monogrammed napkin than this elegant fold.

1. Open the napkin (right side down) and fold in half twice so that the monogram is underneath. Rotate 45° so that the open ends are pointing down.

2. Fold the lower triangle up about 2 cm below an imaginary centerline.

3. Fold this triangle back down along the imaginary centerline.

4. Fold the top triangle down to meet the bottom point.

5. Fold this triangle up again from the center crease.

6. Lay one corner over the other and turn the napkin over.

Dimensions: 45 x 45 cm
or 50 x 50 cm
Materials: cloth napkins
only

ENVELOPE PURSE

The corner of the napkin shown here is beautifully decorated with lace. The design displays it on top and in full view. A menu card may be placed in the pocket.

Dimensions: 40 x 40 cm
Materials: monogrammed cloth napkin or paper napkin

1. Open the napkin (right side down) and arrange it diagonally.

2. Fold both side corners and the bottom corner exactly to the midpoint.

3. Fold the bottom section upward and in half.

4. Fold the top triangle down.

If you own such magnificent lace napkins, combine this fold with equally elegant glassware as your sole table decoration.

LACE FAN

1. Open the napkin (right side up) and arrange it diagonally.

2. Fold the bottom half up forming a triangle.

Dimensions: 40 x 40 cm
Materials: a starched cloth napkin with lace borders or a non-woven napkin

3. Fold the top layer of cloth down from about 5 cm above the baseline.

4. Turn the napkin over and repeat the procedure on the back.

5. At a right angle to the baseline create accordion folds 2 cm wide.

6. Place the napkin in an appropriately sized glass and drape.

ROMAN

Dimensions: 40 x 40 cm. **Materials:** starched cloth napkins, as well as non-wovens or paper

1. Open the napkin (right side down). Fold the two top corners to the center.

2. Fold the lower flap up in the width of the border.

3. Fold the rectangle up to the centerline.

4. Fold the top edge in the width of the border back down to the centerline. Turn the napkin over.

5. Bring both sides around to the front and interlock them. To ensure that the fold does not come undone, fold the corners of the top layers in, forming a triangle.

6. Shape the napkin in a round form and stand upright.

Many napkins have strik-
ing borders which should
not be hidden from view.
This fold was especially
conceived to showcase
them.

Dimensions: 40 x 40 cm or 45 x 45 cm.
Materials: suitable for all napkin types

CORNETTE

1. Open the napkin (right side down) and arrange it diagonally so that the corner with the lace or monogram points down.

2. Fold left and right corners in toward the middle to a distance of about 5 cm from the actual center.

3. Fold the top corner down over the center.

4. Fold the bottom triangle up.

5. Fold both upper corners inward on a slight diagonal.

6. Fold the bottom crease up over these corners and press firmly. Turn napkin over.

7. Bring both sides around to the front and interlock them.

8. Shape the napkin in a round form and stand it upright.

Here is a special fold to showcase unique features like lace or monograms. If the lace is especially pretty it can also be folded somewhat higher (see Step 4).

SWAN LAKE

1. Open the napkin (right side up) and arrange it diagonally, embroidery facing down.

2. Fold both side corners in along an imaginary centerline.

3. Fold the lower corner to the back forming an acute-angled triangle.

4. Fold both sides of the triangle in to the center again.

5. Fold the long triangle point all the way down so that it extends beyond the baseline.

6. At about 2 cm above the baseline fold the point back up.

7. Fold the entire napkin in half vertically, and toward the back.

8. Pull the neck upward at an angle of approximately 70° and fold the head toward the front. Press firmly.

Dimensions: 40 x 40 cm
Materials: starched batiste napkin with Richelieu embroidery on one corner, possibly also paper napkins.

This artistic design appears to float over the table as smoothly and majestically as a swan glides over water.

Small swans can also be folded out of baking parchment.

The ideal couple (right): a beautiful napkin ring and a napkin with Richelieu embroidery. A colorful damask napkin would also be very decorative

LEAF

Dimensions: 40 x 40 cm
Materials: cloth napkins with lace insets or embroidery as well as very sturdy non-wovens

1. Open the napkin (right side down) and arrange it diagonally.

2. Fold the lower half up to form a triangle.

3. At a right angle to the baseline, form accordion folds about 2 cm wide, but only fold one-third of the way up.

4. Insert into a napkin ring and fan open. For greater stability bend the back triangle somewhat to the rear.

TULIP

A low, upright design for which a napkin with crocheted inset was used. A beautiful effect can also created with delicate lace edges.

Dimensions: 40 x 40 cm
Materials: cloth napkin with lace border or sturdy non-wovens

1. Open the napkin (right side down) and arrange diagonally.

2. Fold the lower half up to form a triangle.

3. Fold the right and left corners up to the top middle point.

4. Turn the napkin over so that the closed corner points down, and fold this corner back up to the top.

5. Bring the left or right corners to the middle and interlock them.

6. Rotate the napkin, set it upright and pull down the two loose flaps.

For the Water Lily we recommend napkins in pastel tones. If there is no room on the table for a bread board, a roll can be placed in the middle of each lily.

WATER LILY

1. Open the napkin (right side down) and fold all four corners to the middle. Smooth down all creases well.

2. Repeat this step on the same side and turn the napkin over.

3. Once again, fold all four corners to the middle.

4. Hold down the middle securely and pull out the points located on the bottom, underneath the corners, thereby forming full "flower petals."

5. Pull the corners between the four "flower petals" on the bottom all the way out and bend them upward to form a little basket.

Dimensions: 40 x 40 cm oder 45 x 45 cm
Materials: lightly starched cloth napkin as well as non-wovens and paper

CORNFLOWER

Dimensions: 40 x 40 cm
Materials: cloth napkins, sturdy non-wovens or paper

1. Open the napkin (right side down), fold it in half from the top down.

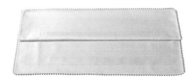

2. Fold the top layer of cloth up to the top crease. Repeat this fold on the back.

3. Starting from the narrow end, create accordion folds, but only along the bottom two creases.

4. Grasp the napkin by the folded edge and tug the front and back layers of material outward. Place the napkin into a napkin ring or an egg cup.

This is a straightforward design which is quick to fold using all materials. The similarity to a Cornflower is especially striking when a blue napkin with narrow lace edges is used.

DOUBLE PEACOCK

Dimensions: 45 x 45 cm or 55 x 55 cm
Materials: heavily starched cloth napkin

1. Open the napkin (right side down) and fold in half from the top down.

2. Fold the top layer up to the top crease.

3. Fold the second layer up, but only to 2 cm below the upper crease.

4. Starting at the narrow end, create accordion folds approximately 5 cm wide.

5. Grasp the napkin at the closed crease. At the other edge pull out the inside layer of each accordion fold to form triangles. Consider ironing at this point.

6. Finally, carefully open the napkin and stand it upright.

The Double Peacock is well suited for large napkins. In the illustration, the border is decorated with tiny loops which emphasize the folds and make it easy to visualize the feathers in the peacock's fan.

PENCIL

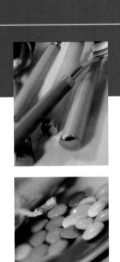

1. Open the napkin (right side down), fold up from the bottom to form a triangle.

2. Starting at either corner, roll the napkin up at a slight diagonal to form a thick tube.

3. Fold the bottom edge into the tube to form a flat stand.

Dimensions: 40 x 40 cm or 45 x 45 cm
Materials: thick cloth napkin with a fringe

An array of colors as seen in this photo is a natural for a children's party. The different colors also make good sense on such occasions because the children can remember which napkin belongs to them.